Discovering
HOW TO MAKE
GOOD CHOICES

Life is full of forks in the road—we need to make a choice at every one.

THE SELF-ESTEEM LIBRARY

Discovering
HOW TO MAKE
GOOD CHOICES

Rita Milios

THE ROSEN PUBLISHING GROUP, INC.

NEW YORK

Published in 1992 by The Rosen Publishing Group, Inc.
29 East 21st Street, New York, NY 10010

Copyright © 1992 by The Rosen Publishing Group, Inc.

First Edition
Printed in Hong Kong
Bound in the United States of America

Library of Congress Cataloging-in-Publication Data

Milios, Rita.
    Discovering how to make good choices / by Rita Milios. —
1st ed.
    (The Self-esteem library)
    Includes bibliographical references and index.
    Summary: Discusses how to make good choices about the
direction of your life, covering such elements of choice as attitude,
identity, and goals.
    ISBN 0-8239-1281-7
    1. Decision-making—Juvenile literature. 2. Choice (Psychology)
—Juvenile literature. 3. Vocational guidance. [1. Decision-
making. 2. Choice. 3. Vocational guidance.] I. Title. II. Series
BF448.M55 1992
153.8′3—dc20   91-31887
                                                              CIP
                                                               AC

Contents

A very important decision for teenagers is choosing the right friends.

Chapter 1
A Lifetime of Choices

Good choices give you ways to be a positive part of

the world.

Decisions, decisions. Every day you make hundreds of decisions. You make both big and small decisions. Decisions determine how your day will go.

You decide what clothes you will wear. You decide what you will eat. You decide how you will spend your free time. These small decisions may affect only one day of your life. It is easy to make these decisions.

You also make bigger decisions. You sometimes make choices that will affect your life for a long time. Choices about drugs, alcohol, or other important issues are not always so easy to make. Choices about how you will spend your adult life are also difficult to make. You may say that you are not making those choices today. But the choices you do make today may affect your future more than you think. You may be making choices that will change the course of your life. Or you may be *not* making decisions. *That* choice may affect your future more than you think.

How many people your age really think seriously about the future? How many know what they want to do with their lives? Do *you* know what you want to do with your life? Do you know what kind of job you might want? Do you know the kind of workplace you might like? Do you know the skills you would need for that job? Do you really have those skills?

Thinking Ahead

At this point it is not necessary that you know the answers to all these questions. You have some time before you need to make career decisions. But you can never start too early to *think* about them. You cannot start too early to think about your *direction in life*.

Who are you? Where are you headed? Those are questions that you should be starting to ask yourself.

High school is a stepping-stone. During high school much of your life is still planned for you. Many of your choices are made for you. But every day you move closer to the time when you will be on your own. Will you be ready to make your own choices? Will you know how to make *good* choices?

What Are Good Choices?

You always make choices. The choices you make decide how your life goes. Bad choices lead toward problems. Good choices lead toward a better life. Good choices are choices that are good for you and for the people around you. They make you feel good about your decisions. You feel good about yourself and your life. Good choices give you ways to be a positive part of the world. They allow you to take part in activities that you enjoy. They allow you to live in a life-style that you enjoy. Good choices are always honest. Good choices always *move you in a positive direction*. They always make your life better.

Bad choices can quickly move your life off track. You probably know of athletes or other famous people who have made bad choices. Their lives went astray. Drugs or alcohol may have been part of the problem. But they had a bigger problem. They did not know how to make good choices.

They did not know how to think about decisions and come up with the best answer. They did not have the confidence to make good decisions on their own. They did not know how to make a positive plan for their life. They did not know how to stick to that plan, no matter what.

Skills That Can Be Learned

Fortunately, those skills can be learned. You can learn to make good choices. You can learn to make a positive plan for your life. You can gain the confidence to follow your plan, no matter what. You can learn to look at the *big picture* of your life.

So often we look at our lives only one day at a time. We do not plan very far ahead. We do not see ourselves as we might be twenty years from now. You cannot *be* where you want to be twenty years from now unless you can *see* yourself there first.

If you can begin to "see" yourself in the future you can more easily make decisions about the future. You can more easily make *good* decisions. If you look ahead you can *plan* for the future. You can plan for the kind of future that you want.

If you look at the big picture you can also learn from the past. You can look back to see why you made the choices you made. You can see which choices were good. You can see which choices helped you in your life. You can see which choices hurt you. You can learn from your decisions. You can learn how you came to make good and bad choices. You can come to understand the *thinking skills* that helped you make good choices.

The choices you make today are in part the result of the *attitude* that you have gained over your life. Your attitude is made up of your thinking *habits*. Your attitude can hold both good and bad ideas. But if you have the *habit* of thinking mostly in positive, helpful ways, you will have a good attitude. And a good attitude leads you to make good decisions.

Learning to think in positive ways, to have a good attitude, is part of gaining good thinking skills. Learning to look at the big picture is also part of it. And learning to make changes when necessary is another part of gaining good thinking skills. When you can think well, you can choose well.

Life Is a Journey

Do you know where you are going? Life is a journey. It is a path. The idea is not to "get" somewhere. The

Good choices are like regular deposits in a savings account—they grow into something worthwhile.

idea is to have a good trip. When you make good choices you have a good life journey.

In the following chapters you will discover how to make good choices. You will read about ways to learn more about yourself. You will find exercises that will help you learn why you make the choices you make. You will learn to think about your choices. You will learn how to take charge of your own decisions. You will look at the big picture of what you want from life. You will be asked to think about what life might want from you.

Decisions such as these are not easy choices. But they are exciting. These are not simple daily choices. They are the kinds of choices that decide not a day, but a life.

Make yours a good life by thinking about your future and planning ahead. Discover how to make good choices.

Chapter 2

Who Do You Think You Are?

You are a part of both your past and your present.

Stop and think a minute about who you are. You will see that you are many things to many people. You are a son or a daughter. You may be a brother or a sister. You are a student. You are a friend. And along with all those "roles," you are just *you*.

But who are "you" really? How are you different from other people? How are you the same? What makes you special?

To know where you are going, you must first *know yourself*. What makes you the way you are? Will you always be the same? Could you change yourself if you wanted to?

You can begin to answer those questions by looking back to where you came from. 13

Looking Back

You are the way you are for many reasons. Your parents helped to make you the way you are. The *genes* you received from your parents make you look the way you look. You may have your father's eyes or your mother's hair. You may be tall like your father or short like your mother.

The place where you grew up also helped to make you the way you are. The kind of home and neighborhood you live in make a difference. Growing up in the city lets you see and experience certain things. If you grow up on a farm, you experience other things. These differences make you see life differently.

Your family and your friends make the greatest difference in helping you to become who you are. Your parents teach you things that they believe are important. They give you *values* to live by. You gain other ideas about life by being with your friends and classmates. You also make your own ideas and attitudes from the experiences you have every day.

Who you are now is the result of all these things. You probably still have many of the same attitudes you had as a child. You may still see the world in much the same way. But that is changing.

Looking at Where You Are Now

Your past stays with you in the values and attitudes you hold. You are a part of both your past and your present. But every day you change. You add new attitudes. You sometimes change old ones. Much of the time you do so without even thinking about it. But it is good to think about these choices.

The more you know, the better you are able to make the right choices.

Will you keep the old attitudes you grew up with? Will you change them?

Old attitudes do not need to be changed just because they are "old." The reason you might want to change some of your attitudes is that they may no longer work for you. They may not be helpful to you in your life today.

Attitudes that no longer work are often the attitudes that you have about yourself. When you were young, you saw yourself differently. You were helpless. You probably were not very sure of yourself. You probably did not feel in control.

As you grew you gained more control over your life. But sometimes the feelings that you had as a child do not change. You may still feel helpless.

That is why it is important as you grow to "update" your feelings about yourself. As you grow more independent, you should feel more sure of yourself. Sometimes to do that you must change some of those old attitudes. You must decide which attitudes about yourself help you today. Which attitudes about yourself hurt you?

You *can* change the attitudes that do not help you. You can change them to new attitudes that help you feel better about yourself.

The first step in changing old attitudes is to find out how you really feel. The "Attitude Assessment" in the next chapter will help you do that. With it you can decide which attitudes about yourself to keep. You can decide which attitudes to let go. That is the first step toward changing old attitudes that do not work into new attitudes that help you.

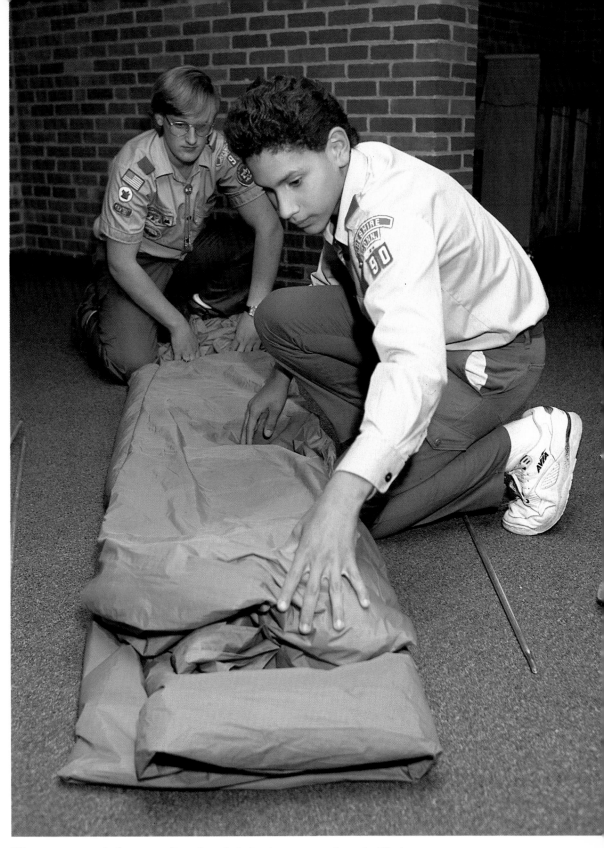

When you are part of a group, its values help to shape your role and attitudes.

Like watching your reflection in a pool of water, reflecting on your attitudes can help you to know yourself better.

Chapter 3

Attitude Assessment Time

By looking closely at your attitudes, you begin to know yourself better.

How do you feel about yourself? How do you feel about your life?

The purpose of this book is to help you get a bigger picture of your life. It is to help you see your future from a wider viewpoint. When you see from a wider viewpoint, it is easier to make choices about your life.

To do that you must first see yourself clearly from where you are now. What are the things that you like about yourself? What don't you like? Do you have old attitudes that are not helpful to you today? What ideas about yourself would you like to change? When you change some attitudes, are you comfortable with them? Do you feel happier?

First let's look at what you *like* about yourself. Below is a list of *traits*. On a separate piece of paper write the words that describe you.

happy	unique	honest	warm
smart	sensible	friendly	fair
strong	positive	confident	caring
proud	clever	skilled	generous
pleasant	kind	fun	cooperative
patient	loyal	sensitive	curious

Add your own words to the list.

Now write a one-sentence description of yourself using some of the words you chose.

You see, you have a lot of things to like about yourself.

But there may be a few things that you *don't* like about yourself. Take a moment to think of one or two attitudes or traits that you would like to change. List things that you *can* change, things that are in your control.

impatient	lazy	unkind	unfriendly
selfish	impulsive	disloyal	intolerant

Now you see that you are a very special person. You have much to offer the world. But you have some ideas about yourself that are not as positive as they could be. That is okay. We all have some bad feelings about ourselves. But have you ever stopped to think about how those bad feelings got there? Do they belong there still?

At some times in our lives we all get *error messages*. These are messages that we think are true at the time.

But we find out later that we were mistaken. Sometimes as children we create error messages about ourselves. We do something wrong and we tell ourselves that we are "bad." Sometimes we receive error messages about ourselves from others. Someone calls us "dumb" and we believe it. The bad feelings from those messages stay with us long after we find out the truth.

If you do not update your attitudes and remove old error messages from your mind, they will always be there. They will make you feel bad about yourself when you really have no reason to do so.

Below is a sample chart to help you assess some of your old attitudes. On a separate piece of paper copy the headings of the chart. Then list attitudes about yourself that you got from your parents. Many of these attitudes you may want to keep. Some you may want to change. Beside each one write "helping" or "hurting" and "keep" or "change."

Next list attitudes that you got from your friends and from school. Which of these attitudes will you want to keep or change?

ATTITUDE ASSESSMENT CHART

Attitudes I got from parents	Helping or hurting?	Keep or change?
I should always do my best	helping	keep
You can't count on people	hurting	change
Attitudes I got from friends, school		
Never be different	hurting	change

A father's negative attitude toward tasks has a large impact on his son's approach to life.

Finally, list attitudes that you got from your own life experiences (good or bad). Which of these have helped or hurt you? Will you want to keep them or change them?

Now look over your chart. Look at the attitudes that are helping you. Those are the attitudes that you want to keep. They help you to feel good about yourself. When you feel good about yourself you act in positive ways. Other people treat you better. Your life is much happier.

Look at the attitudes that are hurting you. Think back for a moment about how you might have gotten these ideas. Could they have come from some error messages? Could some of these attitudes about yourself be wrong?

You can change the error messages. Start by really knowing that they are not true. Perhaps they have some truth. But bad feelings often grow larger than they should. The more you think about bad feelings, the more they grow. When you *pay attention* to bad feelings, you add to them. And every time you have a new problem, you create more bad feelings. These new bad feelings are added to the old ones. Soon you are feeling bad much of the time.

But if you stop and think about the bad feelings, you may find that many are based on error messages. They should not be there. You are hurting yourself when you don't need to. By looking very closely at your attitudes, you begin to know yourself better. You begin to take charge of your own feelings. You begin to control the way you see yourself, your *self-esteem*. You begin to *take control of your life.*   23

Teenagers adopt heroes—people they admire and copy. Learn to choose heroes who are worthy of your admiration.

Chapter 4

What in the World Do You Want?

If a magic genie were to appear before you, what would

you ask for?

What do you want from your life? That is a question that you may never have asked yourself. But it is a good question to ask.

You cannot get what you want in life until you know what it is. You cannot move toward a goal until you have one.

Personal Goals

You probably have some *goals* for your life already. Your present goal may be to get a car. It may be to pass the next big test at school. It may be to find a summer job. These are *short-term goals*. These goals you want to happen very soon. You may also have *long-term goals*. These are goals that will take longer to achieve. Your long-term goal may be to get into a good college. It may be to visit other countries and see the world. You may also have other long-term goals. There is no limit.

Both long- and short-term goals are important. You need long-term goals to have a *vision* of where you are going. You need a firm *picture* in your mind of your future. With this picture, you always have something to move toward. You have to *move toward* something in order to get it.

Goals add *direction* to your life. Long-term goals show you the *steps* you need to take to get there. They break down your big plans into easy pieces. They help keep you on track.

Sometimes you may see only short-term goals. You lose sight of the big picture. Your life is in danger of going off track. If you do not have a clear direction, your life can go in circles. Or it can go nowhere.

Thinking about your goals helps you gain direction. It helps you plan your future. It is never too early to start planning your future. Your "future" really starts tomorrow.

What Do You Want?

What do you want from the world? What does the world have to offer you? If a magic genie were to appear before you, what would you ask for?

Before you set your goals, you must first decide what it is that you really want. What are you willing to work for? What is really important to you?

Wanting does not always mean *things*. Think about *non-things* that you might want too. What non-things would make you happier today? Better health? A stronger body? More free time? A new friend who really understands you? When you think about being happy, "things" are not everything.

Also, happiness does not come only from bringing things (or non-things) *into* your life. It may come from taking things *out of* your life. What things (or non-things) would you like to remove from your life? Stress? Bad grades? Hassles with parents?

Put your wants in writing. Make a list of the things and non-things that are really important to you. List the things that you want to *bring into* your life. List also the things that you want to *remove from* your life.

You now have a better idea of what you want from the world. Now you need an *action plan*. How are you going to bring the things you want into your life? How are you going to remove the things you want to remove from your life? To make these things happen, you must first *set clear goals*. Then you must *create an action plan*.

Let's start with your goals. As we saw, you need both long- and short-term goals. Look at your lists of things that you want to bring into and remove from your life. Which ones can happen right away? Which will take longer to happen? The ones that can happen right away are your *short-term goals*. The ones that will take longer are your *long-term goals*.

Some of your long-term goals will take longer to achieve than others. Some long-term goals may be *lifetime goals*. You may set yourself a goal of being a politician, a dancer, or a doctor. Those goals can stay with you all your life.

Other goals may be years away. They still may not be lifetime goals. You may have a goal of becoming an excellent golfer. You may want to own a business. You might list these as *five-year goals* or *ten-year goals*. By giving goals a *time limit* it helps you to keep on track. You have a target to shoot at.

Listing your goals is a useful tool. But it is only a tool. Listing goals does not lock you into your plans. It gives you direction. But you can always change that direction. If you see that some of your goals no longer interest you, simply *change them.* Just remove them from your list.

No goal or plan is set in cement. As you grow and do new things, you may change your mind many times. You can change your goals as often as you like. The only way you can go wrong is to have no goals at all.

Setting Short-Term Goals

Begin to think about your future by deciding on your short-term goals. Make a list of your short-term goals *in order of importance.*

Now look over your short-term goals. Which ones are most likely to happen? The ones that are easiest to achieve? Perhaps. But more likely it is the ones at the top of your list. It is the goals that are *most important* to you that you are most likely to achieve. Those are the goals that you want most. Those are the goals that you have the most reason to work toward.

It is always good to think about the importance of your goals. If a goal is not really important to you, will you want to spend your time and energy on it?

Teenage love is romantic and exciting, but it calls for responsible choices.

An action plan helps you to spot obstacles and find ways to overcome them as you work toward your goal.

Will it take up time and energy that you could spend on a more important goal? As you get older, there will be more demands on your time. Job, family, friends, and outside activities will all take up time. You may have to give up some goals to have time for others. Knowing which goals are most important to you will help you to decide what to let go.

Decide what you are willing to do to make your short-term goals happen. Remember, *it is up to you*. If you do nothing, nothing happens.

Creating an Action Plan

You now have a good idea of your short-term goals. You know which are most important to you. To make them happen you must *do* something. Think about how you might go about reaching those goals. Think of any problems that might come up. Think of ways you can overcome those problems. Make a copy of the chart below and fill it in to use as an *action plan* for your short-term goals.

Goal	Problems	Ways to Overcome	Action Plan	Date Taken
			1st Step	
			2nd Step	
			3rd Step	

Reaching a long-term goal requires dedication and practice.

Chapter 5

Thinking Ahead

What really big goals do you want to reach for?

Once you have made some good decisions about your short-term goals, it is easier to make long-term goals.

To make good decisions about your life, you need to know where your life is headed. You do not have to have an exact plan for your life. You just need to know the *direction* of your life.

So let's begin charting some *long-term goals*. Instead of starting with the closest, let's start with the goals that are farthest away—your *lifetime goals*. Sometimes it is easier to decide on a "final" goal and work back. Then you know the goals you will need in between.

A Lifetime Goal

As a teen, the last thing you are probably thinking about is old age. But try for a moment to put yourself very far into the future.

Imagine yourself at your grandparents' age. Imagine looking back on your life. How would you like it to have been? What kind of work would have kept you interested for thirty years? What special talents would you like to have developed? What dreams would you want to have had come true?

Perhaps you can talk with your grandparents or other older people. Ask what things they are happy with about their lives. What are they glad they did? What do they wish that they had done? What changes would they make if they could?

Then think about yourself. You have talents. You can prepare yourself to use them. Or you can push them aside. Maybe you will never get around to using them.

The decisions you make today *do* make a difference. Do you have goals for your life? Do you have an action plan? Without goals, without an action plan, your dreams will never come true. Every successful person has goals. Every successful person has an action plan.

Begin now to form your own long-term goals and action plan. Both will probably change many times. That is okay. Changing a plan is very different from having no plan at all. When you change a plan, you still have *direction*. You are headed somewhere.

Use your imagination and make a list of a few lifetime goals. Think about your talents. Think about your dreams. What really big goals do you want to reach for? Think about non-things as well as things. All your goals will show how you feel about yourself. They will also show how you feel about your place in the world. The time to think about lifetime goals is *now*. Now is the time to start making them happen.

What Do You Have to Offer?

It just makes sense that you cannot get things free. Even goals that are non-things do not come free. There is always a price. But the price is not always money. Often the price we pay for getting what we want is *time*.

We have only so much time in our lives. How we spend that time is a very important decision. How will you spend the time that you have? Will you spend it doing things just for yourself? Will you spend some of it helping others?

Doing things that *help other people* helps you to get what you want. When you help other people, others want to help you. We all need the help of others. We cannot do everything alone. Being the kind of person who likes to help others brings you friends. And friends can always be counted on to help you.

Your Gift

Each person has his or her own special gift. Each person is *unique*. You have talents that no one else has. You have certain ways of doing things that are yours alone. You have a special way of seeing the world. Only you have *your* special gift.

Each person offers something different and unique to the world. What do you have to offer that no one else has? What can you do *for* the world?

What are your *natural talents*? How can you use them to help others? To make the world a better place?

Make a list of some ideas. List the natural talents that you have. They do not have to be "big." They do not have to be talents like dancing or singing. Perhaps

35

Perhaps your special gift is getting along with older people.

you get along well with older people or very young children. Perhaps you are a good listener. List the things that *you* feel you do well. Beside each one list ways you might use that special gift(s).

Keeping on Track

Now that you have looked at the big picture of your life, you can better see the smaller picture. You have a vision and a direction to guide you.

Now use that vision and direction. Think about your "middle goals"—your *ten-year, five-year,* and *one-*

year goals. By working *back* you can get a better idea of how to make these goals happen.

You have an idea of where you are headed. To get there, where might you have to be in ten years? For instance, say your lifetime goal is to travel all over the world. You want to use your talent for finding your way around strange places. You want to explore the world. You also want to experience many new customs. You want to share your experiences with many people.

Look at that bigger goal. Think about the kinds of things you might need to have done *ten* years from now. In ten years you would need to have visited many countries. You would need to have had money to travel. You might have needed to find jobs in other countries. You would have needed to speak to the people. You might also have needed to learn new languages.

What kinds of things would you need to have done *five* years from now? Where would you need to be? Still in your hometown? How would you get where you should be? How would you get the money? Would you need to have learned a new language?

What kinds of things would you need to have done *one* year from now? Taken advantage of school? Studied a foreign language? Gotten a summer job? Saved some money?

Make a list of some of your possible ten-year, five-year, and one-year goals. Make them fit *your* dreams. Make them up if you have to. Have fun with it. You can always change your plans. Remember, the only wrong plan is to have no plan at all.

An action plan for getting a job can start with checking the want ads in the newspaper.

Chapter 6

Getting There from Here

Each day you can do something to *move forward*

toward your goals.

Just by reading this book you have made it more likely that you will achieve your goals. You have begun to *think ahead*. You have begun to *plan* for your future. Doing the exercises in the book helps you even more. It helps you to figure out in your own mind what you want.

Now that you have come this far, what's next?

Taking the First Step

Right now you are still *getting ready* to take charge of your life. You are not yet on your own. You might think that there is little to do right now. You might think that you can't do much until you are an adult. But that is not so.

Each day you can do something to *move forward* toward your goals. Life is always moving. If you are not moving forward with life, you will soon be moving backward.

Look at your one-year goal(s). What can you do *today* to help you move toward that goal? You do not have to get far. Just *move forward* toward your goal.

To move forward today you may need only to do something as simple as going to school and doing your best. OR there may be other things that you can do. You might be able to get some information that you will need later.

Say your one-year goal is to have a part-time job. Today you might begin looking in the newspaper. You might look at jobs for people your age. You can get ideas of the kinds of work you might do. You can also make a list of possibilities. You can ask older friends where they work. You can let them know when you will be able to work. You can ask their help in finding a job.

Help!

Don't be afraid to ask for help. Most people like to help others. Most people will be happy to help you. But they do not know when you need help. You must *ask* for it.

By asking for help, you let people know what you need. They can then tell you when something comes along that might be right for you. But if you do not ask, no one will know to help you. Ask friends, teachers, counselors for help. You will find all the help you need—if you ask for it.

Making the Most of Your School Counselor

Most schools have *counselors*. The counselor's job is to help you. School counselors can help you with almost any kind of problem. You can go to them with personal problems, school problems, or friend problems. Counselors will listen to you. They may have the answers for you, or they will tell you where to go to get the answers. Sometimes they can help you find your own answers.

Your school counselor is a gold mine of ideas, information, and resources.

School counselors can also help you to decide on plans for your future. It is a good idea to go to your school counselor well ahead of time. Let him or her know that you are thinking ahead. Tell your counselor your ideas. Ask help in making plans. The counselor can help you to decide on the kinds of classes to take. He or she may be able to help you find a part-time job or school/work program, or plan for college. The counselor can help you best if you ask early.

Help From the Community

Often you can get help from leaders in your community. Many schools have programs in which community leaders talk to students. They tell about their work. They help students decide if they might like that kind of work. Sometimes community leaders let students visit where they work. Students may spend one day or several days. They can get real job experience and know what to expect.

Ask if your school has a community program. You may want to join it. If your school does not have one, you might help start one. You can learn about jobs. You can make friends with community leaders. You can move toward your goals. It all starts when you *take action*.

Self-Discipline is very important to goals. Self-discipline means that *you* make sure that you do what you set out to do. It means that you are responsible for your actions. *You* take charge. You do not depend on others to remind you. You keep *yourself* on track. You *make yourself* meet each goal.

Self-discipline is not easy. It is not easy for adults. It will not be easy for you. But with self-discipline *you are a winner.* You become more capable. You become smarter. You become more confident. Self-discipline is worth the effort.

But I Can't...How many times have you *not tried* to do something because you thought you couldn't? Don't let your dreams stay dreams forever. Make them real. You can *if you think you can*.

Start small. Pick out one *small* thing to do. Then do it. Make that appointment with your counselor. Ask an older friend for advice. When you have done that one small thing, you can do more. You will find it easier to take the next step. You can build on your first success. You have learned to do something new. You can build on what you have learned. Go ahead. Try it!

It's All in Your Mind. We have been talking about goals—small goals, large goals. Goals help you to be successful. Success is doing what you want to do. Success means have a goal and reaching it. And the key to reaching your goals is found *within your own mind*.

Sometimes to get what you want, you must first begin to *think differently*. It is not enough just to do something. You must *be confident* about what you do. To move forward with your dreams, you must be confident in yourself.

Confidence is an attitude. It comes from *your thoughts*. The thoughts you think can make you confident. Or they can make you feel not good enough. It depends on the *kinds of thoughts* you think.

Do you think confident thoughts? When you try something new, do you think, "I can do this"? Or do you think, "I'll never make it"? You may be surprised at how much difference your thoughts can make. Thinking *positive thoughts* helps you succeed. It helps you to reach your goals.

Positive thoughts are thoughts that make you feel more sure of yourself. Positive thoughts are thoughts of confidence. Positive thoughts are "I can" thoughts. They are thoughts of self-acceptance. They are thoughts of *knowing* that you are good enough, smart enough, strong enough.

Negative thoughts are the opposite. Negative thoughts are "I can't" thoughts. Negative thoughts take your confidence away. They leave you afraid to try new things.

But the good news is that you can control these thoughts. *You control all your thoughts.* So you can *decide* to think positive thoughts instead of negative thoughts.

It may not be easy at first. You may have grown up thinking negative thoughts. But *positive thinking can be learned.* It is a *habit.* You can learn to think positively by trying it for a while. Then it will become a new habit.

When you find yourself thinking, "I can't," *change* the thought to one that can help you instead of hurt you. Change it to something like, "I know it will take some work, but if I try, I can do it. I can always ask for help."

You see, the way you think is *your decision.* No one else can think for you. If you take charge of your

Like completing a jigsaw puzzle, reaching a goal brings the satisfaction of a job well done.

thinking, you take charge of your life. Deciding to think positively is a good decision. It usually leads to success.

Keep your thoughts *on* the good that is in your life. Take them *off* what is wrong in your life. Choose to think about what is right about you instead of what is wrong. Hold in your mind a picture of yourself *having achieved* your goals. Let this *vision* be your guide. All successful people have such a vision. They always *move toward* that vision. You can, too.

Chapter 7

The Path of Life

You can create your life the way you want it to be.

Your life is a journey. The goal of life is to *experience* living. It is to try to make the journey a good one.

Each day that you live, you are going down a "path." But it is not a path that leads to a place. It is a path of decisions. It is a path of choices. How you make *each choice* decides where you go next.

Every person travels on his or her own path. Every person travels alone. You must learn to make your own decisions. You must think for yourself. You must learn how to make good choices.

Your Path

Where will your choices lead you? Where will your life go? It is up to you. You alone decide your path.

You decide where you are going by the choices you make each and every day.

It should be clear to you by now that you have an opportunity. You can create your life the way you want it to be. You can live your dreams. You alone are responsible for the choices you make. So, in the end, *you alone are responsible for your life.*

Which path will you follow?

Will you make use of your natural talents? Will you let them go to waste? Will you choose a career that will help others? Or just yourself?

Those are the kinds of choices you will make. You would be wise to think carefully about such decisions. They affect your whole life. They affect whether you will be what the world thinks of as successful, having lots of money and the "good things" of life. They affect whether you will take the path of doing good in the world, choosing one of the "helping" professions, or making it possible for others to have good lives of their own.

It is not easy at a young age to see the big picture of your life. It is not easy to imagine the best path. But you do not really have to have all the answers. It is enough that you *ask the questions.* It is enough that you *begin to think* about the answers.

For it is in the *experience* of *looking* for the answers that you will find the answers.

The answers may change. They may be different tomorrow from today. But just by *thinking* about them you point yourself in the right direction.

Your path will become clear if you simply *move forward toward the vision* of your goals.

As the backpacker decides on the trail to follow, we set our own path through life by our choices.

Life is something like a chess game: The winner is the one who plans several moves ahead.

Chapter 8

A World of Choices

By learning to "think ahead" you learn to make better choices.

The world will soon be yours. You will go out into the world to find your "place." You will give your special gift.

The gift you give can be big or small. You may influence many people. You may help save lives. You may help young people or old people. You may help one person or you may help many. It does not matter. What matters is that you give *your* special gift.

You can become almost anything that you want to be—if you try hard enough. You can have more than one job. You can play more than one role. You can do as much as you want. When you know that you are in charge, you can do almost anything.

Planning Ahead for a Career

You still have several years before you will begin a career. Yet even while you are in school you should be thinking ahead. You should be thinking about what you are going to do after school.

The world moves very fast today. Things change faster than they did in your parents' days. Research and technology have made the world a different place. The future is not as certain as it used to be.

Your parents may have done the same work for a long time. If it is work that they like, they may want to stay at it their whole working life, but that is not often the case. Companies make changes more often than they used to. Then often the workers must change their plans too. Today's workers change jobs more often.

In the future when you go to work, people will probably change jobs even more often. You need to think ahead about what kinds of work you would like to do. You need to have more than one idea.

Using School to Gain Job Skills

Soon you will need to know how to get a job. You may even be looking for a part-time job right now. You may already be in need of some good job skills.

Job skills are the things that you need to know on a job. Some job skills are just for one job. They are the special things that you need to know about the work you do each day. Sometimes you learn these skills on the job, such as running a machine or using special equipment. You may also learn these or other job skills at a college or technical school.

Listening to people who have experience of the world can help with making good choices.

But there are other job skills that you can learn today, right at school. School helps you get ready for your future. Many of the things that you learn in school will help you later when you have a job.

If you work in a building trade you will need to use math skills. Carpenters measure things. They add and subtract measurements. If you work as a salesperson, you will use math to figure out prices and add up orders. You will also use some of the things you learn in English and sociology. You will need to speak correct English. You will need to understand people and why they are like you or different. Every day, you will use the skills you learn in school.

School teaches you other things that you will use on your job. School teaches you about responsibility. You must be at school on time every day. If you are not, you must make up for your mistake. You also must do your homework and study for tests. If you do not, you will have problems. Learning to be responsible for your own actions in school will help you to be responsible on your job. It will help you to get to work on time. It will help you to do your job right.

At school you also learn to get along with different people. You learn to accept authority. You learn to work in a group. All these things help you to be a better employee later in life.

In school you learn to make choices about your life. By learning to "think ahead" you learn to make better choices. You learn to make choices that can help you for a long time, not just today. You can learn the *habit* of making good choices. You then can take that habit with you wherever you go.

By thinking ahead, you may decide that it is good for you to go to school every day. You may decide that it is a good idea to be on time. You may decide that it is a good idea to do your best and learn as much as you can. You may see the *long-term* good that this will do for you.

Can you think of other ways that school will help you with your long-term plans? Make a list for yourself of ways in which school helps *you* get ready for your future.

How a Job Changes Your Life

When you think ahead, you may begin to think about the kinds of jobs that you might like to do. You may think about the things that you do well. You may start to think about how a job will affect your life.

When you get a job, you don't get just a job. You get a *change in life-style*. You get a *workplace* that is different from home or school. You get *different kinds of people* to deal with. You get many new *responsibilities*.

It is good to think ahead about some of these changes. Thinking ahead will help you decide which changes you might like. It will help you decide which changes you would not like. Then you can better know which kinds of jobs you might want to do.

For instance, you may have thought that you would like to be a dentist or a dental assistant. But after thinking more about this *workplace*, you may decide that it is not right for you. You may like working closely with people. You may like to solve problems and help people. But you may not like to stay in one place all the time. You may not like to stand all day.

55

If you get a kick out of reading to your little sister, you might make a wonderful teacher.

You may like to walk around and go different places.

By thinking ahead you can decide what things you *do* like about this kind of job. You can decide what things you *don't* like. Then you can look for a job that can give you more of the things that you do like and fewer of the things that you don't like.

Questions to Help You Decide What You Like

Ask yourself these questions: Do you like working with others? Do you like working alone? Do you like working inside? Do you like to work outside? Do you like to be told specific things to do? Do you like to make your own plans? Do you like to work with your hands? Do you like to think and solve problems? Do you like to work with machines? Do you like to work with papers?

Asking yourself those kinds of questions will help you get a "big picture" idea of the kind of workplace you would feel good about. It will give you a better idea of the kinds of jobs you might like. If you do not think ahead, you may have to try many jobs before you find the right one. Or you may never find the right one.

Think about the kind of work and workplace that you might like. Answer the questions above and make a list of others to help you.

Keep Your Options Open

At this point in your life you do not need to make a decision about the work you will do. You just need to begin *thinking* about it. It is good to think about *types* of jobs rather than *specific* jobs. Think about "building trades" rather than carpentry. Think about "medical services" rather than nursing. That way you have more *choices*. You have a *direction*. But you are not stuck with just one possibility.

The world is always changing. When you are ready for a job, there may be choices open to you that are not here today. By thinking and planning ahead you will be better able to look at those options and make good choices.

Whether you are thinking about a job or just about what you will do after school today, you will always do better if you think ahead. If you start today, you can learn the *habit* of making *good choices*.

Glossary

action plan An idea or ideas about how to go about doing something that you want to do.

assessment An evaluation or study of something.

attitude Ideas or feelings that stay in a person's mind and affect other ideas or thoughts.

big picture The view from far away or far into the future.

error message A mind message that is not correct; a mistaken way of thinking.

job skills Skills or abilities a person needs for a job.

life-style A way of living; a pattern of daily life.

lifetime goal A plan for something a person wants to do that will take most of a lifetime to achieve.

long-term goal A goal that is not possible to achieve immediately.

negative thought A thought that hurts you or moves you in a negative direction.

positive thought A thought that helps you or moves you in a positive direction.

role A way of acting or being.

self-esteem A good feeling about yourself.

unique Not like anything else.

values A set of ideas to live by.

vision A mental picture or image to strive for.

For Further Reading

Alvyn, M., PhD. *TA for Teens*. Jalmar Press, 1979. A book for teens about taking control of their feelings and making their own choices. Illustrated.

Carson, Richard D. *Taming Your Gremlin*. New York: Harper & Row, 1983. A book about anger and other unhappy feelings and how to make choices to reduce them. Illustrated.

Cohen, Susan. *Teenage Stress*. New York: M. Evans Publishing, 1984. How to make choices that keep stress out of your life.

Laubach, Frank. *Changes*. New York: New Reader
Press, 1982. Two short stories and two
biographies about Helen Keller and Martin
Luther King. Illustrated.

Le Shan, Eda. *What Makes Me Feel This Way?* New
York: Macmillan, 1972. How to deal with
emotions and decisions about growing up.
Illustrated.

Sheperd, Scott. *What Do You Think of You?* Compcare,
1990. A book about self-esteem and making
choices about your feelings.

Smith, Sandra Lee. *Coping with Decision Making*. New
York: Rosen Publishing, 1989. A book for teens
about learning to make your own decisions.

Van Wie, Eileen Kalberg. *Teenage Stress*. New York:
Julian Messner Publishers, 1987. How to cope in a
complex world.

Index

About the Author:
Rita Milios is an author, speaker, and educational consultant. She has written thirteen books, among which are *Discovering How to Make Good Life Choices* and *The Value of Trust* published by The Rosen Publishing Group. Her other books include early readers, nonfiction books on science and values issues, and adult psychology. She often speaks on the topics of self-esteem, creativity, and the use of the mind.

Ms. Milios lives in Toledo, Ohio, with her husband and two school-age children.

Acknowledgments and Photo Credits:
Cover photo: Stuart Rabinowitz
All photographs by Dru Nadler.

Design and production by Blackbirch Graphics, Inc.